I0212318

Now We're Truly Beautiful

A Collection of Poetry and Spoken Word

Now We're Truly Beautiful

PJ

PHOENIX JAMES

NOW WE'RE TRULY BEAUTIFUL

Copyright © 2025 Prince-James Harrison.

All rights reserved.

No part of this publication may be reproduced,
distributed, or transmitted in any form or by
any means, including photocopying, recording,
or other electronic or mechanical methods,
without the prior written permission of the
publisher, except in the case of brief quotations
embodied in critical reviews and certain other
noncommercial uses permitted by copyright
law.

For any questions about usage, please email
contact@PhoenixJamesOfficial.com

First Edition: 2025

ISBN: 978-1-0685383-1-5 (Paperback)
ISBN: 978-1-0685383-2-2 (Ebook)

Cover Artwork & Design by Phoenix James.
Book Design & Formatting by Phoenix James.

Visit the author's website at
www.PhoenixJamesOfficial.com or email him
at phoenix@PhoenixJamesOfficial.com

DEDICATION

To those
Who found themselves in darkness
Who were lost and alone
Suffering in silence and pain
Torn apart amidst the chaos
And the carnage
Deafened by the screams
And the laughter
Suffocated by the destruction

Those who loved
So freely and deeply
How naively we fall
Eventually we're crushed
And eaten up by it all

And to a loving young boy
Who discovered himself
In that darkness
And silenced all the suffering
And the pain he felt within
Who tore apart all that chaos
And the carnage they left him in
You finally opened your eyes
And then tightly held your breath
Until you suffocated all their voices
Which returned you to your depth
You quietened down all the noises
Setting your mind and spirit free
I hope you too are feeling empowered
To see how beautiful now are we.

CONTENTS

A BETTER IDEA OF LOVE

That I should write
A book about love
A book of love poems
Purely on love
Is a nice idea
It's a nice thought
But on further reflection
I honestly don't think I'm qualified
To write anything
Other than mere musings
On the idea of love
And my thoughts on love
And my opinion on love
I would definitely say
I'm no expert or authority
On the subject of love
And what love is
And what love means
And what love is supposed to be
That would be the day
My muses
Would have to work overtime
To produce such a work
Through me

And let's hope they have a clue
Let's hope
They can shed some light
That might benefit someone else
On what love means
And what love is
And what love should be
And how love should be navigated
Because all of the things
That I thought were love
Are not
At least not my idea of love
Or perhaps they are
And I've got it all wrong
About my idea of love
And if so
Then I still don't know
What love is
Because I am unable
To recognise it as love
So again I say
It's a nice idea
That I should write a book
Purely of love poems
But I don't feel qualified
I don't feel I would be doing justice

To those who open the pages
Hoping to be inspired by
Guided by
Excited by
The true meaning of love
The true expression of love
With that said
I could probably write
A good few books
On what I think it should be
What I think it should look like
How I think I would feel
When I felt it
When I saw it
When I experienced it
But then I would still question it
Whether or not
It was true love
Or just my fancified idea of love
Or whether
I was merely
Being duped by someone
Who had an idea
Of what another
Should perceive love as
That sounds scary

I don't love the idea at all
I'd probably do a much better job
Of talking about
All the things
That love hasn't been
What love isn't
What love should be
Than pose as any authority
On what love actually is
And I love that
A whole lot more
As the better idea.

ALL THINGS IN TIME

That took a while
To understand
That I don't have to
Be present in everything
And not everything
Requires my presence
Which then gives me more time
Also realising
That everyone gets
Twenty-four hours
To do
To manage as they want
And once I realised those things
It kind of made me relax a bit more
About running out of time
And being on this hamster wheel
To earn money
To be
To get ahead
To maximise
All of my opportunities
I found
It made more things
Come to me

Than when I was chasing
When I just allowed myself
To just be
And accept
That there is more than enough
Time to achieve
What I have to achieve
And also
Putting things
Into compartments of time
To manage my goals
Pretty much like a type of schedule
Organising helps
What I'm going to do
When
And how long for
And how much I need to achieve
If I want to do this hundred things
In a year
But I haven't got any plan
For what I'm going to do
Each week
Or each month
Or each year
To do that in a year
But actually breaking down

How much I would need to do
In a week
A month
To actually complete
That hundred things
By the end of the year
Having that kind of plan
Took away
Some of that anxiousness
That we have
About time running out
And having to do this
And do that
Do a hundred things
And to-do lists
It took away a lot of that
Realising that if I just relax
If I just do
This seven or this ten things
In this amount of time
I could double that
In double the amount of time
And if I continue
In that that space
I will achieve
What I set out to achieve

Within this amount of time
And it made it very simple
And less crazy
Than if I just had
One hundred things
And no idea
When I was going to be doing what
To get to this end goal
That kind of also helped
And realising
That so many people
Have done so much more
With less
Also helps
Because I often like to look back
And see
What other people have achieved
Who didn't have what we have now
Like, for example, just the internet
And the speed that we have
With the internet
A lot of people
Did not have that
So they had a different system
For achieving
What they wanted to achieve

And reaching people
And all the rest of it
So time was different
So understanding that
Helped also
Time management, I guess
And managing the tasks
Into bite size chunks
There's a saying
About eating an elephant
It says
How do you eat an elephant
One bite at a time.

BEDTIME AS A KID AND NOW

Imagine that
We didn't want to go to bed
When we were younger
We had to be forced
To go to bed
Our parents said go to bed
And we wanted to stay up
And to watch something on TV
And we were warned
That it was scary
But we didn't listen
We just wanted to stay up
And then we got scared
And we didn't want to go to bed
And go into the dark
But then we had to go
Because by then
It was really time for bed
Way past our bed time
But we didn't want to go to bed
We wanted to stay up
When there were people over
And people chatting
We wanted to be up

We wanted to be part
Of the excitement
We didn't want to go to bed
We never wanted to go to bed
As far as I remember
And now, look what's happened
Now we're all grown up
Now, we can't wait
Now, we're happy
When people leave
So we can go to bed
Now, we can't wait
Now, we're not interested
In anything but the bed
Clean sheets
Warm and cozy
That feeling
Of getting into clean sheets
There's nothing like that feeling at all
Who thought
It would have come to this
When we were kids
And then, now
We don't want to get out of it
When we were kids
We couldn't wait

To get out of bed
And go do whatever it was
That we wanted to do
We were up first
Before everyone else
Out of the bed
Doing whatever
Now we don't want to get out of bed
We're crying
Do I have to get up
What a way it's turned around
We're terrible.

BRAND NEW FOOD PALATE

I'm definitely one
For new experiences
In everything in my life
I believe in trying everything
When it comes to food
I am willing to try things
I've not tried
Even more so now
Because my diet has changed
In the past year
And I'm a lot more open
To eating things
That has led to me being able
To eat things I couldn't eat before
So I definitely would try things
Rather than close myself off
To trying things
That I may not know what they are
Or what they're about
Or anything like that
I'm not that person
I'm the person that would try
And if I don't like it, I don't like it
If I like it, I'll have more of it

And the other thing
My addictive personality
Would also lead me
And once I do find something
That I really like
I would want more of that thing
So that may be the only reason
I don't try more of other things
Because I found
The thing I really want
And I just want to taste that
That can happen too
But I would try everything first
To find that thing.

BROKEN HEARTS: NEW & USED

It was nighttime in the city
I saw what looked like a homeless man
Rummaging around in a dumpster
He had a huge sack
On a two wheeled trolley
It was filled to the top
Packed with broken hearts
He was collecting more
And just tossing them
Into the sack with the others
I still think about that night
And what it meant
I don't think there was a time
Where my heart was whole
But I at least wish you'd met me
Before it was this fractured
This broken
This frail
I wish you'd met me before
Before and after the warnings
Before the sirens
Before all the noise
And all the screaming
Before all the pillows

And the mattresses
Suffocated us
Before the unwanted pregnancies
Before the births
Before the kidnappings
And the hostage situations
And negotiations
Before all the plans of attack
And all the escape plans
I wish I'd met you
Alone
On my solo expedition
On my way back to the war
I wish the sun stayed shining
I wish the nights never came
I wish I wasn't so hot
I wish it wasn't so dark
Of course
I was destined to explore
But I know for sure
You would have had the words to say
To make me walk a different way
I know you would have believed in me
Enough to whisper away my naivety
And a whisper
Is all it would have needed to be

Maybe that's just fantasy
Far away from what I'd believe it to be
Or maybe in actuality
That would've been reality
Perhaps the gods
Have been merely challenging me
With bad dreams for my eyes to see
Preparing me
For the big reveal
Where the hopeless curtains open
To all that I've ever been hoping
At the grandest ever show
Or perhaps we'll just never know
But I prefer never to think so
To just defer or relinquish hope
Though I don't think
I'll ever be able to let it go
How they try to take everything from you
And then say it ain't so
How they try to rip your heart out
And destroy your soul
I don't think I would know
How to even start to let it go
How the darkness takes hold
Grips you
And takes complete control

Splits you apart
And makes you feel cold
And alone
Breaks your heart
A little more to know
No-ones ever coming home
To help, to heal
Or so it feels
And that's never pretty
It's a sad, sad pity
Like nighttime in the city
Seeing what looks like a homeless man
Rummaging around in a dumpster
Carrying a huge sack
On a two wheeled trolley
Filled to the top
Packed with broken hearts
While collecting more
And just tossing them
Into the sack
Along with all the others
And I look on now
Still thinking about that sight
That scene
What it's all about
And what it means.

CAPTURING THE FLOW

It could go either way
I could be really inspired
By what's happening at the moment
The relationship I'm in
The vibe and the energy
Could be that muse for me
To make the flow
Of writing come more
Or it could be
That I'm more isolated
And not around anyone
And then have more time
To delve into those thoughts
Inside my mind
And create from there
Which could produce even more
More creative flow
Could come out that way
It really depends
And it could go the other way as well
Where the relationship I'm in
Is not really giving me anything
I'm not feeling inspiration from it
To write anything

Or I'm not feeling in a creative space
Or that person is not being conducive
To that muse environment
Not them being a muse
But the space I'm in
Becomes the muse
With that person
With my life
And us together
It could be taking away from it
It could be sucking the life out of it
Depending on who I'm with
And the vibe
And what's going on
Or I could be on my own
And I'm just not really feeling anything
In that way
That I really want to document
At that time
That's how it would have been
At one time
But now
It seems to just flow all the time
Whereas there may have been times
Where I feel I needed
Some kind of action to be going on

To be able to create from
I don't have that anymore
It's just a constant tap now
Hence why I'm so focused
On capturing
What I'm capturing right now
I'm just not focused on being on the road
Not focused on doing other things
Outside of the writing
And the publishing
Because this flow is happening
And I just want to keep capturing it
With my buckets
And this flow
While the water is turned on
While the flow is going
Because you don't know
It might just turn off
I don't think so
But you just want to kind of
Capture it while it's flowing
That's the state I'm in right now
That's why I'm actually
Onto the next book, and so on
That's the space I'm in now
I don't see that turning off right now

But because it's there
I'm just going with it
I'm just going with the flow
As they say
There's never been a truer time
In my life
Where going with the flow
Has been more relevant than now
There's a lot of creative flow happening
And I'm just capturing
Capturing, capturing, capturing
And it's great
It's a really great time
And long may it continue to flow.

CLEAN STREETS OF TOKYO

I'll tell you one place
That really surprised me
Was Japan
It was a beautiful place
The people were very nice
I had a lovely time there
But one of the things
That I was not expecting
Was how clean the streets were
So very clean
I've never seen anything like it
In anywhere that I've been
There's always been
A discarded soda can somewhere
Some used tissue paper
Just blowing around
I did not see anything like that
In the streets of Japan
It was so clean
It was very surreal
I've never seen anything like it
I don't think I'll ever have
An experience like that in London
Or in England

This was Tokyo for me
And by the way
It wasn't too clean
As in too much
It was beautiful
It was nice
I just don't know
How they maintain it
I guess people just don't drop litter
In the way that we do here
And other parts of the world
It was good to see
It's nice to look out
And not see the streets
Covered in rubbish
And mess
And to see
That it can be done
This was another thing
That showed me as well
We can keep our streets clean.

DEPTH AND INTENSITY MATTERS

The interesting thing
That I think gets overlooked
When someone says
They've been with someone
For this or that amount of time
When the relationship
Was this long, or that long
I think what's not taken into account
Is how much time
Those people are spending
Around each other
For example, one couple
Have been together six years
And this other couple
Have been together six years also
But the first couple
Have lived together
In the same house for six years
While the other couple
Saw each other every weekend
It's going to be a different relationship
The two relationships
Can't be classed the same six years
Six years of living in the same house

With someone day in and day out
Is very different
From six years
Of spending the weekend together
Every weekend
It's two different levels
Of connection
And tolerance
And communication
It's just a whole different relationship
So when people say
We've been together
For such and such amount of time
It depends
There are nuances to all of it
Me and my ex-girlfriend, for example
We didn't live together
But we spent a lot of time together
So practically
If I wasn't at her place
She was at mine
So if we were making that trip
Away from one house
We'll be making it together
To the next house
So the together time

Was the same as living together
Although we did it
From house to house
It wasn't like
We were going our separate ways
For a week
And then meeting back up
At the end of the week
And just talking on the phone
In the middle of the week
That's a different relationship
I find that interesting
It's important
To have that frame of reference
That perspective
To understand
Or have a view or idea
On what type of relationship
It was, or is between people
Although
The quality of the relationship
Is not limited to
And can't always be determined
By just 'together time' alone
Depth and intensity in the relationship
Are factors to be considered

And not to be overlooked also
Regardless of
The amount of time spent
In each other's presence.

FEELINGS OF BEING LOVED

Hello, she said
I hope you are keeping well
Knowing you're very busy
And your time is very calculated
I didn't want to disturb you
Calling you at the wrong times
But I'm just wondering
If you have any free time tomorrow
I want to see you
Even just for a while
In the coffee shop
If you're busy
Your gift I got for you
Has been here with me
For two weeks
Since you haven't texted me back
And we don't even talk much
To each-other
Like we used to sometimes
I don't know if all is okay
I feel a little confused
I have never been into casual dating
As it's never been my kind of thing
Please don't get me wrong

I'm not trying to force you on me
Or intending to put any pressure on you
I really don't know how you feel about us
Meeting each other
But I feel great
And willing to know you more
And tell you everything about myself
So you know me
It's not just physical attraction
But I feel a sense of belonging
In your arms
Every kiss
And touch
Talks to my soul
I don't know yet just what it is
I can't say
But it feels so good
And natural
As if it's meant to be
I do understand
If you feel nothing like this with me
And I will never force myself on anyone
Or cause pressure of any kind
But I would like you to know
Your small, heart-warming
Kind, loving gestures

Our communication
Flowed like never-ending
Amazing feelings of making love
My body shivers
Feelings of being loved
Or cared for
You coming to see me off
On the platform
Sitting on the bench
In the middle of the busy high street
Yet getting lost in each other
And you asking me
If I want any dessert
And taking me to the shop
It meant the world to me
As I hardly remember
Anyone doing that for me
Rather I was the one
Asking and doing it for others
Last time
You telling me
I'm safe there
I feel it so much
That every time
My eyes tear up just remembering it
It means a great deal

To hear those words
And to feel safe
For a woman who has been abused
All her life by people
Who are supposed to protect her
Now if you wish to cut me off
And you feel I'm not your type
That's absolutely okay
I'll for sure be a little sad
And wish we could see more together
But I'm already thankful
For this experience
You have given me much
Without asking
In a very short time
And I forever appreciate
And cherish our time
If I don't hear from you
Then I will take it as the message
I will be sad
But I will be happy for you
Knowing you're with someone
That you're more happier with
I have missed you a lot since
It's a very strange feeling
I don't know

I just don't know what it is
Feelings are just feelings
They know no boundaries
I have felt a lot for you
Nobody else
I'm not a woman
Who follows her vagina
But I have been longing
To feel my soul
Which you made me feel somehow
I will wait to hear from you
Whatever it is for you
I wholeheartedly appreciate the truth
Well, take care of yourself
Much love.

FUTURE WE

I often think
About contacting you
Yet I am still afraid
I shall explain
I'd be taking a huge step forward
After years and years of relationships
With women
Much
And I mean much too much
The wrong choice for myself
And I, I would say, wrong for them too
But that's not the problem
I have endured a lot
In those long years
Giving chances
Wanting it to work
But here I have given up
I am at peace on my own
But the leap of faith
I have been taking
Dating again
Is still early
As I have to put my thoughts right
In other words

What I've been thinking is
I would like a serious relationship
Which would build up slowly
But surely
And to reach this
Both the man and the woman
Have to ensure
That the boxes
Are ticked in, to achieve this
I have often worried I'm getting old
Only to realise
It's becoming the opposite
Which which fills me
With much optimism
I have been with good intentions
And successful in them thus far
To change my diet
My old habits
To return to the gym
I am pleased with progress
Those around me notice
And commend and applaud this
Tell me I do not need it
But my mirror told me I did
I wouldn't consider me a 'party boy'
But I can entertain a whole room

With my charisma
I love music
Dancing
I'm not a professional
But I have all the rhythm
Wish I did more with it
The second important thing for me
Or I should have put it at number one
Is my religion
I am an artist
Another devout rebel of the world
Genius level creativity
And prolific
There's much to show and share
And I guess equally plenty to to tell
Perhaps for when we meet
But that creative nature
Is rooted in my DNA
I know you'll understand it
That and my God are one
My mind is more open now than ever
From experience
I have learnt that it is important
That both people in a relationship
Have the same faith
Or can relate to one another's

It's not as common
In relationships
As one would expect
Hope
Or desire
As being yoked to unbelievers
Is a disobedience to one's self
And a necessity to be yoked
If both share the same faith
I don't know what your age will be
If you'll be younger
Or older than me
Not that it matters too much
Right now at least
I have vowed
That I will never
Make the same mistakes again
Though since then
I've made the error of repeating them
I'm making them much less now
As I did as a younger man
Will you want to start a family
If we do so decide
By such time
I hope it's a thing
We can both supply

I feel otherwise
It might make one
Or both of us
Feel inadequate
Useless perhaps
And preventing the other party
From having their desire for such
The hurt might be too much
The straw that breaks the camel's back
Will you want promise of marriage
Who knows
We haven't even met
Once in a while
My faith in such regards
For a brief time, is renewed
By someone I've been close to
But mostly by the thought of you
I've been torn
I've been burned
I've been broken
For the simple reason
I only wanted to be married once
I was always the boy of the fairytale
When you become him
He's hard to leave behind
Which of the two of us will die first

Leaving the other behind
To the emptiness of what was
To the loneliness
Of what can no longer be
Will we want to marry again
And have still a family
Why not
There's nothing wrong with that
I'd encourage it to be
If it is you I should leave
Here to exist without me
Perhaps rather a conversation
For after we at least meet
Please do excuse me
Seated in all that's been wrong
Reasons
For never ever
Wanting to be married
And all the lies
And the broken promises
The lies and the deceit
And the pain
That hurt so much
That it is beyond words
I am now healing
Trying not to look back

Yet not wanting to misstep
By having chosen to forget
Hence, corresponding here
To start to reach you
Is what I would be happy to do
To start that journey
I am open and transparent
As there's no point in pretending
Or glossing over the truth
For in the long run
What good does it do
So, I hope you'll feel comfortable
With what I am saying to you
Wait, what am I saying
It's you
I know you will
I know you do
I know you know
That there are children to be freed
And we are all and each free agents
Grown but still in need
And no need so much to be polite
I believe that everybody here
In this place
Is looking for something serious
Or at least something meaningful

Which is not built overnight
Hence it is best, in this case
Not to hide anything from you
Nor you from me
When we do eventually meet
Rather than expose our truth later
And end up both displeased
Wanting to break free.

HIGHLY RECOMMENDED

Over the past few days
I've somehow
At very different times
And in very different situations
Been fortunate to meet
And be in the company of
Some really cool characters
And we've together
Found laughter
And made huge
And hilarious jokes
Out of some of the smallest
And silliest things
I wish I could run through
Each of the scenarios with you
Or draw you pictures
Or better still
Put you right into those moments
For you to experience them too
I have truly laughed so much
Until my sides hurt
And I couldn't breathe
Even now
I can still feel my sides a little

And flashbacks
Of some of those discussions
And exchanges
Are still making me chuckle now
I laugh often
But I seriously
Haven't laughed this much
In a while
I'm sure you can recall
A time when
You laughed just like that
Laughter is truly
A great feel-good medicine
For all things
Many say it's the best
It's also very infectious
I definitely recommend it
Highly
If you feel
You have nothing
To laugh about
Just laugh at me
And share the joke
It's great to laugh.

HOW TO BECOME INVISIBLE

When I was younger
I wanted to have the power
Of invisibility
I used to watch characters
In cartoons and television shows
Turn invisible
And wished
I could turn invisible too
I used to imagine
All the things
I could do as an invisible boy
Unfortunately
Or perhaps fortunately
I never acquired those powers
Until now
I say to you
If you haven't already
And you ever want to experience
What it's like to be invisible
Just simply
Throw on the magic outfit
Wear a simple high visibility vest
And go down
To any busy high street

Or public area to test it out
It works instantly
You will not be disappointed
On Thursday
We completed shooting
For a little short film
Titled, 'A Contribution'
In which I play
Lead character, Michael
A street cleaner
Who finds being the person
Who is constantly judged
Due to his job
Is no fun.

IN THE GAME

In the game of life
We can sit
On the sidelines
All day long
Calling ourselves
Competitors
And point fingers
At the field
And criticise
The actual players on it
About what their doing
And how their doing it
And what they should be doing
Or not doing
Or could do better
Like a lot of people
Choose to do
It's safe
It's easy
And in many cases
A great way
Of diverting criticism
From ourselves
Making us feel better

About our own shortcomings
However
I personally find it
Far more fun
Challenging
Exciting
Rewarding
And empowering
Being in the game
Playing the game
Enduring the trials
Highs and lows of the game
Whilst learning the game
Growing from the game
Meanwhile
Staying in the game
With my eyes on the game
It's really hard to score
When you're not even
In the direction
Of your field
Much less your goal
So, eyes on the ball
And keep it moving.

IN TIME SILENCE HEALS

You say
Please talk to you
That you can take
Anything I give you
Throw at you
That I should express it
That is how we heal, you say
Or if I'm seeing someone else
Other than you, you ask
And if I want you
To leave me alone
Then fair enough
You're very respectful
To another's decision
But you need to hear from me
For your own healing
You want to know
What this connection meant
For me
To just tell you
Whatever it is
If it was just a casual date
Just great sex
Or was there more

What hurt me
Or if I need space
To tell you that too
You'll wait
As long as I need time
That you're a grown woman
Though you behave, you say
Like a bitchy child.

LET'S TRY GETTING OFF

It's been an interesting
And enlightening
Educational and fun
And exciting journey so far
And I'm sure it will continue to be
For as long as I'm in those spaces
What I love
Is that it's something
That allows you to connect
With people
You might not otherwise meet
In this fast paced world
Of everybody hustling and bustling
And to and fro
And never having time
And everyone's face glued to a screen
I find that it's great for connecting
It serves its purpose
Connecting people
And that's how I try to use it
Purely for that
Not to stay on there
And take up residence
But instead

When I connect with someone
I like to move the connection
Off of there
As soon as possible
And into what I call
The real world
Like having a phone conversation
At a very minimal
Not just texting characters to a screen
I think it's great
I think it's perfect
It's just a way to connect people
And everyone's face is
Like I said, in a screen these days
So it works
But it's not a place to stay
It's not a place to build that connection
It's a place to just make it
And then expand that connection
Off of the app
Off screen
How have I found it
It's been great
It serves its purpose
It is full of a lot of shifty people
It is time consuming

It is hit and miss
It's a god forsaken place
In a lot of regards
But again
If you use it
The way I feel it should be used
Making the connection
And getting off of there
As soon as possible
Until you need to be there again
To make new ones
I think that's the way it works
The way it should work
And then it's all fine
It's not such a god forsaken place
Because you're not there
Long enough to notice
Then you're back in the real world
You're meeting people
And making connections
And actually speaking to them
Pretty early on
After the initial match
And then
You're just seeing the world as it is
People are good, people are bad

People are good for you
Not good for you
People are compatible
Not compatible
And you're in the real world
You're not in this app
Where it's like, what the hell
And the time it takes
To go through
All of these profiles as well
And the back and forths
And the texting
You don't notice it as much
If you don't spend
As much time there
Doing that.

LITTLE WHITE GOOSE

I hope
You write the book on your life
The one before birth, to now
You said, last week
You were thinking
Of turning your story into a film
And true, where would one start
And where to publish the book
It'll take you perhaps a year, you say
Maybe, who knows
It's your first
And you want to write it yourself
Not by a scribe
The way it should be, I always say
Your first poem was at fourteen
When your grandfather died
Then you wrote a series of other ones
You say what you find difficult
When writing the book
Is the tense to use, past or present
As if you are sailing through the years
Or projecting yourself in the past
Hence using the present
You wondered if I understood

I do
You say that perhaps
You've found a guide in me
And this is the reason you picked me
Without knowing
You watched me in Egypt
And in the film on the flight
You say you used to work for an airline
And dated a pilot
Who you found out, after he died
Was a secret agent
For the United states Air Force
Who was infiltrating
The airline you worked for
To obtain information
On arms trafficking
You had the flight plans
And you helped him to investigate
Without knowing
What you were doing
I hope this will all be in your book
Of course, you will not be able
To use your name
As there's some sensitive information
Which could jeopardise your existence
If it was revealed

A story that implicates
The Luxembourg government
Enough now, you say
As you're treading on dangerous territory
You recall you were taken hostage
In Beirut during the coup in the seventies
I agree, you're not the little white goose
You may appear to be
With the ability to switch
From one personality to another
Depending on the circumstances
You, like me, understand people
The poor, the rich, the murderers
And the innocent
Those who are locked in prison
And those on death row
You corresponded with a man
For years, in Texas
And when you didn't hear
From him anymore
You knew he had gone
To better lands
I agree, you should translate
A few of the lines
Of the poems you wrote in French
Even though

They won't rhyme in English
Laughing is good for your health
So say the Japanese, you say
I also agree it's weird
How a sad poem
In a different language
Once translated
Becomes hilarious
And tears of sorrow, in French
Rolling down one's cheeks
Become the result
Of laughing excessively, in English
You say you love the films
That I've been involved in
Also my expeditions in Egypt
You've been six times
But you don't fly anymore
As when you worked for Cargolux
In Luxembourg
You were involved
In several traumatic experiences
One which, in your life
Was the turning point for you
You were caught in a massive storm
In layers of cumulus clouds
With lightning at its origin

You couldn't divert West
Because the control tower
Were not responding
To give you permission to do so
And you had to face the music
The sound of the radar
Becoming overpowering
As you approached the beast
You were all silent on board
Captain
First officer
Flight engineer
And yourself
In the cockpit
Trying to contact the control tower
Begging on the radio
Charlie Victor 892 calling Beirut
Beirut, do you read
To no response
Just cracks
And unbearable high pitch sounds
In the headphones
You strapped yourselves
Waiting to pass from reality
To the real reality on the other side
You find it therapeutic to talk about

58

As this experience
And being taken hostage
In the desert in Lebanon
Have marked you for life
It's why you don't fly anymore
It's called 'the fear of flying', you say
Yes, indeed, it is a shame
Let's hope they find another way
Which has an anti-crash immunity
But then, even flying saucers crash
And their technology
Is much more advanced than ours
So it's hopeless, you say
You tell me that your book
Will be full of sorrow, joy, crazy stuff
And unbelievable true experiences
And that you can't wait to read it
After you finish writing it
How you may surprise yourself
I can't wait to see your book too
Writing, I agree, is a good way
To project your most secret thoughts
Things you would never know
Were there resting, as you say
At the bottom of your brain
I think and say this all the time

Which, when you write
Are vomited onto the page
Or the screen
As one's fingers
Can't go fast enough
To produce the evacuation.

MADDY PLAYS THE BADDIE

Maddy was just nineteen
He was twenty-three
Now she
A young twenty
He
Laid a seed
Her
Now mother to be
Expecting quadruplets
But it gets more complex
He was married
She didn't know
Wife now pregnant also
The plot thickens
She is with twins
This husband and wife
Will take
The four additional babies in
Maddy is due to give birth first
She can't wait
For that special date
To give the four newborns away
To the expectant couple to raise
She just wants to get her life back

To those previous days
Of being young
And having fun
Hooking up
And going on dates
Late nights
Swiping right
And getting laid.

MY ECLECTIC TASTE IN MUSIC

My taste in music
I could tell you that I like folk music
I could tell you that I like R&B
I can tell you that I like rap
I can tell you that I like reggae
Rock, soul, classical, opera
My taste is very, very eclectic
I could probably tell you better
What I don't like
More than what I like
Because what I like
Is so much more
Than what I don't listen to
And that is techno and heavy metal
Those are the two genres of music
That I don't listen to
What do I listen to
More than others
Presently
I would say
Soul and hip hop, probably
At the present moment
Modern soul more so
And modern hip hop

Neo soul
But I go through phases
Where I would be listening
To a lot more reggae
Than what I'm presently listening to
And then, there'll be another phase
Of another genre of music
That I listen to a lot more
At that time
So it changes
It's not that way all the time
Out of that whole set of genres
It changes quite often
And it still will probably depend
On what artists
I'm listening to at that time
Or what's influencing me
At that time
Right now
I'm listening to a lot of neo soul
Which I'm quite enjoying
So many different styles of music
That I'm inspired by
Yesterday
I was talking about opera
And one of the classics

That I enjoy in that genre
Classical music too
I listen to a lot of jazz as well
I listen to a lot of instrumental jazz
Saxophone jazz, piano jazz
I like a lot of that
I play that a lot, actually
If there's any genre
That I play the most
It's probably that, jazz
Yeah, more than anything
I'm going to have some jazz playing
In the background
Regardless of what I'm doing
I like jazz.

NEVER BEEN MARRIED, THANKFULLY

I say thankfully
I've never been married
Because the majority
Of my experiences of it
Not having been married myself
Just from observation
Have not been great
The majority I've seen
Have not been good experiences
For those people
And the people
That I speak to
When I get the opportunity
I say to them
Would you do it again
And not one of them have said yes
So that's my view of it
And I say thankfully
Because I wouldn't like
To be in their position
Having spent all those years
I mean, they don't regret their children
Or anything like that
But they say they wouldn't marry again

Basically, if they went back
The children is a separate thing
They would still have the children
But they wouldn't
Have the marriage again
No way would they do that again
If they could do it with the child
And without the marriage experience
They would do it
But if it's just the marriage
And not the child
They wouldn't do it
So that's why I say
Just one example
Why it's not something
I'm aiming to do
And it's not something
I feel I've missed out on
Because of observation
And the way of the world
I think the world has changed
Compared to what marriage was
And for good and bad I think
But the world has changed
In regards to the meaning of marriage
And how it was back in the day

So much has changed
But one thing hasn't changed
A lot of people these days
Are opting not to marry
And I think for similar reasons
And the ones that were married
Are now not married
And there's so many divorces
The divorce rate is so high
And that just doesn't appeal to me
That doesn't make me excited
About getting married myself
Every other person I speak to
Is going through divorce
At the moment
And wouldn't do it again
I've seen so many others
And so many disasters
And heard so many stories
My parents didn't stay married
My grandparents
They didn't stay married either
And my great grandparents
Didn't stay together either
But they did it
Like everyone else

Had the marriage
Had the children
Had the relationship
That didn't work out
And then
You see it outside
Of your own family
You see everyone else
Not having a great time
You see it not lasting
So I don't think it's necessary
For one thing
I say this countless times
Over and over again
I say that the marriage
Is not the day you say, I do
That's not the marriage
Or at least it shouldn't be
But a lot of people think it is
Which is why I think it doesn't last
Because the marriage
Needs to be already established
Before you even say, I do
For it to even have a hope of lasting
The marriage needs to be more
Than just a day of, I do

And more than the vows
It needs to be something
That's not even visible
Like, okay, the day is visible
The church is visible
The wedding dress is visible
The ring is visible
The groom
And the bride are visible
The best man
And the maid of honour
And all the bridesmaids are visible
The flowers are visible
The cake is visible
But the marriage
What is actually marriage
Is not something you can see
It's something that needs to be there
Already firmly existing
Before you take the vows
The wedding day
Should be nothing more
Than a celebration
Of an already existing
Strong secure marriage
A solid union between two individuals.

NEW PROVERB

Don't

put all your eggs

in one bastard.

NO LESS THAN EXTRAORDINARY

Nothing I've done
Hasn't been extraordinary
I wouldn't be anywhere
Where I am now
Without having have gone
That extra ordinary way
It just never would have happened
In the way that it has happened
If I hadn't been that way
It takes that
I wasn't doing ordinary things
I was performing on stage
Three times a night for a long time
Different places
Not in one place
I mean from one place
And then on to another venue
Then to another venue
And I did that for years
Spoken word poetry
That's not ordinary
That's extraordinary
That's beyond
What is probably generally expected

Maybe one show a night
It's probably not expected
To even do one show a night, really
Unless you're a full-time artist
Touring nonstop
All year round
I was doing it at that level
So that, that's not ordinary
It's no different
Than any touring artist
Vocalist, or musician
Stand-up comedian, and so on
I'm standing on stage
And performing poetry
It works in the same way
The touring is the same
Practising your set is the same
When you've got new material
You want to try out with an audience
Whether it's an audience of fifty
Or an audience of fifty thousand
Or even if it's just five people
It's the same
It's no different
At least that's the way I treated it
Other people

May have a different experience
But that was all I knew
Because I was around singers
And musicians
I was around comedians
Who were all travelling and touring
And doing just that
I didn't come in from a literary door
From a literary background into poetry
I was a singer on stage first
With live bands and musicians
Then I was a rapper in a group
With live DJs
Then I performed my lyrics
Without music
I came into it
Through performing
Around people on stage
That's all I knew
I didn't go to 'poetry readings'
Until after
I only knew live showcase events
Where you were performing
With all kinds of other artists and acts
Who were there to entertain an audience
None of them poets

None for how well they wrote a poem
I came into those circles later
I was more Hackney Empire
Places like that
Singers nights
Comedy shows
Music festivals
Gala events
Club nights
Radio stations
That's my experience
So I treated it like that
Touring from city to city
Touring around the country
Out of the country
Performing with other artists
And bands
I was the poet on the bill
That was my journey into it
I only knew it that way
So very early on
I was doing extraordinary things
For a how most
Would imagine a poet
I would say.

NOW WE'RE TRULY BEAUTIFUL

Sometimes
It's me
I have flaws
I'm not perfect
Do we all heal
Over time
With the right person
Or are we all
Just
Ticking time bombs
With feelings
With boundaries
I have one for you
Maybe I'm scared
Of the growing feelings
Not knowing
What you are
Or how you feel
About me
Really
Where I stand
As we never clearly
Talk about it
Not really

I never knew
I would feel this for you
This soon
I didn't plan anything
I should act more like a kid
Less like an adult
Like you
And talk to you
As that person
Rather than
Sending messages
That say
I'm serious about you
I'm very sorry
But maybe I'm scared
To ask
In fear of pain
Hurt
Rejection
I think of distancing
To better save me
I don't know why
I'm so anxious
So needy
And seeking attention
From the anxious

And needy
Attention seeker
I'm a respectful person
I respect myself too
I follow routine
I have a disciplined life
I'm a happy person
I never judge anyone
On just one event
But I don't see
Honesty in your eyes
Your smile
Your words
I need to calm down
What could turn to anger
To real rage
Let myself heal
Your pain
As well as mine
Maybe I cause you more
Talking
Over the phone
Messages
In person
Whatever
What do you feel like

Now
But a bad idea
Please don't leave me
Just like this
But I wish you would
Completely
Sometimes
I think about killing you
But I'm to busy for prison
I value my time
My life
And my freedom
More than the satisfaction
Of revenge
For five minutes
I'd question all my life
Why I wasted it on you
I hope you find forgiveness
In your heart
For all who've hurt you
I'm pretty sure
You hurt them too
With an evil smile
And would again
If you could
We are all human

Full of emotions
I do wonder though
If the ones
Who have no belief in god
Like you
Are different
Than the ones who do
To have no fear
Of judgement
Of consequences
Or karma
You healed me
From some already
Sometimes
I see you
And want to say
Thank you
And I no longer
Have expectations
I am free
So very free
And I ask you
For nothing more
So beautiful indeed
Now
Are we.

ONE PART EMPATHY

Feeding too much
Of your energy
Into empathy
Will end up
Leaving you empty.

OUR DIVISIVE DEVICES

I think we've become
So attached to technology
And robotics
And smart devices
That our brains work in that way
Although we're not genetically robots
I think our brains work that way
I think we operate robotically
With all of this technology
And smart devices
And all of this computer stuff
That we rely on
I think we are part that
For the simple fact
If it all stopped for five minutes
We'd all be messed up
Without it
We wouldn't be able to function
Doesn't that sound like a robot
Like, if we lost our smart phones
Or we couldn't get onto the internet
Or suddenly
Our microwave wasn't working
Or whatever it is

That we use the most
We'd be stuck
Without whatever device it is
That we're attached to
I think in that sense
We are part android now
In a lot of senses
Or you could even say
In a large part of our senses.

PEOPLE, THOUGHTS & THINGS

Surround yourself
With people
Thoughts and things
That continuously
Uplift
Motivate
Drive and inspire you
Remind you
That you are greater
And stronger
Than your situation
Or circumstance
Show you
That there is magic
And a lesson
In every moment
Encourage you
To believe
That you can always
Do
Learn
Grow
Achieve
And become more.

QUEEN OF SERVICE

I was at the airport
In the duty free area
And I was checking out some fragrances
Some colognes and aftershaves
I was looking for a couple in particular
I then came across a fragrance shop
And so I went in
I received assistance
From a young male
Who identifies as a female
Clearly I could see
That he was dressed more feminine
Than masculine
And was very feminine himself
He spoke that way also
His name was Alex
And I was along with it
For the whole time
I always speak to people
How they like to be spoken to
And addressed
And so on, and so forth
Pronouns, and all of that
Throughout my time

In the shop
He gave very good customer service
So that was one of the things
I commented on
While finally making my purchase
And then at the last minute
When I was asked
To fill out an electronic form
Some customer feedback
On how I'd rate his customer service
How I thought the service was
That would go to his managers
As I was typing
And giving him all the compliments
And all the praise
Saying how good
The customer service I received was
What I typed was 'he'
Referring to him
For whoever was going to read it
I remember him receiving
The machine back from me
Looking at what I'd typed
And then changing it to 'she'
It was funny to me, in the moment
Because it hadn't crossed my mind

To type 'she'
As I didn't actually know
How he identified
I just knew he was a young male
I did apologise
Obviously he didn't take offence
He was very gracious throughout
But it was just one of those moments
Where you're reminded
You have to be kind of on the ball
It's a different world now
It's a very different world
I've never had any problem
With anyone who identifies
As something other than
What they were assigned at birth
I'd like to say
If I'd been thinking about it
That I would have typed 'she'
Instead of 'he'
But that would have been presumptuous
Naturally, I saw a young guy
Who presented himself
In a more more feminine
Than masculine way
He clearly dresses

And carries himself as a female
In every way, I would say
At least on appearance
And the way he spoke
It's just one of those
Funny things
That can pop up in your day
That was far from one's mind
It just made me think
What an interesting world
It has developed and progressed into
I can't even begin to imagine
What other wonderment
And progressiveness
The future has in store for us.

SAD IN A LITTLE WAY

It's sad to think
That we're only
A blip in time
Like a raindrop in the ocean
In regards to how long
We'll exist time
Time is a vast ocean
And we're only a raindrop in it
We won't get to see
All the world
All the beauties
Of the whole planet
We won't get to see half of it
There's so much to see
So much to experience
And we couldn't possibly
See all of it
So we'll miss so much
During our very brief stay
Our trip almost seems wasted
For how much we won't see
We arrive and depart in a day
Life doesn't let you see it all
It's kind of sad in a little way.

SELF CARE NOTICE

When we fail
To confront the things
That bother us the most
And simply
Shoo them away
With illusion
Or temporary distraction
They seemingly disappear
And leave
Only to emerge
From some dark underworld
Every so often
To disparage our existence
And torture us.

SINCERE PROPOSAL

As a new year begins
And another one ends

I have just one question
To you, my lovely friend

Would you let me hit it raw
And never call you again.

SUCCESS STORY

A woman
I was speaking with
Said, let me tell you a story
She said, on the surface
Everybody is happy
For you to succeed
They see you
Working very hard
Towards your goals
And ambitions
And wish you well
While you are
On the road
To succeeding
She said, but not all
Of those people
Really want you
To actually succeed
That many of them
Are hoping
You won't succeed
And would be happier
And more satisfied
Within themselves

If you fail
She said, the successes
Of others
Frightens these people
It forces them
To examine
Their own inadequacies
In regards to
Where they are
On the road
To succeeding themselves
She said, not everybody
But these types
Of well wishers
In particular
Don't believe
You'll actually get anywhere
With your enormous goals
And grand schemes
And dreams
So they're very happy
To wish you well
But when you surprise them
And you actually succeed
Well, she said
That's a different story.

THE ART OF COOKING

Do I like cooking
Yes, I do like cooking
When I'm doing it
I like it when I'm doing it
I don't like it before or after
I like it because I like creating
And cooking for me, is creating
And experimenting
And trying different recipes
And different seasoning
And ingredients
Adding, and taking away
Creating something
I believe in tasting the food
Throughout the process
So you know exactly
What you're going to end up with
So that is always a joy for me
And reaching that successful end
Something that I could actually palate
It's not something I do often
But when I am doing it
I enjoy it in that moment
Of actual creating

And getting to a place
Of making something
Artistically edible
Artistically edible in the taste
The taste has to be
A creation I've crafted
I've creatively put something together
And it's a masterpiece
In terms of how it tastes
It's a successful creation
Often, it's my own recipe
It's a work of trial and error
But I enjoy that process
Of getting to the place
Where it tastes amazing
Because I've just gone through
That whole process
Something doesn't taste right
It needs more of this
Or more of that
I like that whole thing
That's the creation for me
But if I didn't have to cook
I wouldn't do it at all
I don't do it
Because it's a passion of mine

But I enjoy it when I'm doing it
Because I'm a creative soul
I get involved
The other thing
I wouldn't do
If I didn't have to do it
Is I wouldn't eat
If I didn't have to eat
That's how much
I could just leave food
Altogether
I could not do it at all
And be content
It's not that much of a thing for me
If I don't have to
I much prefer not to do it
Having someone cook for me
Is always a great luxury
That I wouldn't say no to at all
That means I don't have to do it
I often look for ways
To cut down the process
Of me preparing a meal
I would get something from the store
That doesn't require much preparation
Or I would have a takeaway

But takeaway
Is probably the least
Of the things I do
One of the biggest things I do
Is batch cook
And that would be the thing
That stops me
Having to cook more
Than I would want to be
So I cook once
In a batch
Whenever possible
That would last me
Over the period of the week
And I don't have to return
To the cooker at all
And I'm not opposed
To the odd ready meal
That I can just put in the oven.

THE HAIRDRESSING YEARS

When I left school
I began working for a salon
Cathy's Hair World
In East Ham in London
I began working with her
And her all female team
Doing hair there
I did all sorts
Everything you could possibly do
With hair
I was doing more
On the female side initially
But I only got into it
Because I wanted to do barbering
I'd started doing my own hair
From age eleven
I was very good at cutting hair
Because my mum thought it'd be cheaper
To get me the clippers
She got tired of doing it
And I got frustrated with her
Not doing it to my satisfaction
So I started doing it myself
Learning, making lots of mistakes

And then became a very good barber
And then wanted to do it professionally
This is all in the early nineties
All before the internet took off
And the how-to videos online
On how to do a high top fade correctly
Or do a Nike or Adidas or Fila logo
Designed into someone's haircut
This is from years of practising
On my own hair
And growing my skills
And my confidence
I went and studied at Newham college
Got my Men's Hairdressing certificate there
I passed a thirty-six week course
In just eight weeks
Because I'd long already had the skills
I was very impressed with myself
Later on, I went to another salon
In Tottenham in London
Audie's Professional Hair Studio
It's not there anymore
I was told that the only route
To becoming a barber
Was through doing women's hair
I was young and naive

And didn't know better
And they, as a business
Had greater plans
To meet the needs of that business
More than my own
And at that time
Required me to do more
On the women's hair side of things
Looking back on it now
The men's side was definitely covered
They already had a few amazing barbers
And only one main women's hair stylist
So they pushed me towards that
Saying I had to learn women's hair first
Rather than just go to the barbering side
I didn't know any better
So I did a lot of women's hair there
Eventually I got the opportunity
To demonstrate my barbering skills
And was considered qualified
I learned a great deal from both
And appreciate those opportunities
That served to shape me
In so many other areas of my life
So that's kind of how my start was
Leaving school

And going straight to work
And then later on
I developed into doing more barbering
And I wanted to branch off
And to do my own thing
I then managed a salon
In Hackney in London
Doing predominantly men's hair
And barbering, as I'd originally desired
And continued with that for a while
Then after I went more into the arts
As in what I do now
I've had all the styles on my own hair
I've had all the styles imaginable
I've had locks
I've had short hair
I've had blonde hair
And all the colours you could think of
When Sisqo from Dru Hill was popular
I did that whole thing too
With the platinum colour hair
And then I had fuchsia coloured hair
And orange hair, and green hair
All types of short styles
I had the skinhead
I had the big afro

All the high top fades possible
I had the Tupac Shakur high top style
When he played Roland Bishop
From the movie Juice
I had that style
I had so many different ones
I went through so many different phases
And styles of hair
I don't think there's a style I didn't have
I had the waves
I had Jhery curls, S Curl
And all types of curly perms
Everything
Extensions
Cornrow
All kinds of plaits
All of it
I don't think there's a style
That I haven't had.

THE SOUND OF SIRENS

I'm reminded
Of something I watched yesterday
A black man, Charles Ramsey
Living on Seymour Avenue
In Cleveland, Ohio
He'd moved to the neighbourhood
Just two years prior
And was a neighbour
To a guy named Ariel Castro
And it turned out
In the end
That this neighbour, Ariel
Had kidnapped three girls
And held them hostage in his house
And Charles
One day
He heard this loud scream
And this, now a woman, and two others
And a young girl
Were locked in that next door house
He managed to get the door open
For the three women and the girl
To escape the house
And to contact the police to come

And it all got solved thanks to him
It was found that Ariel
The kidnapper
Had these girls
Held captive in the house
And had got one of them pregnant
Over the period they were trapped there
Charles said
He used to see the baby in the yard
And thought
It was just the granddaughter
Of Ariel, not knowing
It was the daughter of one the girls
Ariel had kidnapped
And had held captive in his house
For ten years
And had impregnated
It was a whole thing
It was crazy
But there was this one other thing
I had noticed that stood out to me
Quite often, as people do
I read the video comments
And someone there
Had commented underneath
On that same thing that I'd noticed too

When Charles
Was outside with the news reporters
And the police had arrived
And were co-ordinating
And everything was sealed off
And the whole neighbourhood was out
To see what was going on
With all the police vehicles
And the cameras
And all the excitement
And the commotion
In the heat of it all
A police car siren
Suddenly went off in the background
Nothing unusual
Based on the circumstances
Probably just turning up to the scene
Manoeuvring through the crowds
Or leaving the scene
When this happened
Charles kind of jumped
And he looked around
And then continued talking to reporters
The comment underneath the video
Mentioned how Charles jumped
When the siren went off

I didn't even think
That anyone would actually
Even pay attention to it, like I did
But it made me think
Yes, he's black
And there's a police siren
And about how
We're almost programmed
As black people
To react in that kind of way
When we hear one
Because even if we're the ones
That called the police
In the first place
We still don't know
What's going to happen
When they arrive
And police are around us
That's what it made me think about
How it's definitely in us
To have that initial reaction
To that sound
Because our experience is
That the police
Are not necessarily coming to help you
Even if you're the one that called them

That's what it made me think about
In that moment
And then further
After seeing
That someone had also noticed it
He was just returning home
With some McDonald's at the time
He was having a Big Mac
When he heard the loud scream
And he said, what made him look
Is because all the kids stopped
Because they heard the loud scream too
He said he thought a tree
Had fallen on someone
So he came out to investigate
And discovered it was the woman
Trapped inside Ariel's house
Trying to get herself out
From the locked door
She was trapped behind
Charles Ramsey was credited
For rescuing the three women
And the young girl
Who had all been kidnapped
And held captive by Ariel Castro
In his home for ten years.

THE WARMTH OF US

You send me pictures
From the park
And other naked photos
You thought were so..
Inappropriate
That you deleted them
They looked ugly, you say
Compared to those beautiful ones
You'd taken previously
You hoped I'd understand
What you were trying to say
Some thoughts
That you'd send me again
That it was too much for one day
So not to overload my brain
With things like that
Said you'd send me everything
With a promise
You reminded me
I was your book
Your safe harbour
You send me a dress you love
Because it reminds you
Of our Christmas together

Your mind, you say
Looks exactly the same way
As my wall
With all those little sticky notes
The main difference
Is that everything is messy
And in different shapes
That my wall looks organised
And every note has its place
You love it, you say
And that we never had
Our morning coffee
And our noons
But we had everything else
My leg, your leg
My arm, your arm
My smile
And the warmth of me
Who made you laugh again
They say
Two clever people
Can't fall in love
You say
That true love
Needs one idiot
That there is always one idiot

And that idiot is always you
But you don't mind it, you say
If I make you smile
If I make you feel special
If I make you listen to music
If I make you spread your wings
Fly, and dream again
To then let you be that idiot
That it's better
Than being nothing
Or no one
You say you wanted to ask me
So many questions
You wanted to explain
So many things
But when my lips kissed your lips
You forgot about everything
All those unanswered questions
Still haunting you
My leg, your leg
My arm, your arm
My smile
And the warmth of me
My look, your eyes
My touch, your hug
My kisses

And the taste of your lips
You've waited for my kisses
One year, one month
And twenty days, you say
And that no wonder
You forgot everything
That you wanted to ask me
When you kissed my lips
You say you've lost yourself
In my kisses
But being lost in my kisses
Was the best thing
That happened to you
For the past one year
And it was worth waiting for.

THIS TOO IS POSSIBLE

It is quite possible
That some day in the future
A group of people
Are going stumble
Across someone
Who is doing exactly
What you've done
And are doing now
And will all tell the world
How amazing
And unique that person is
And what a genius they are
And that there has never
Ever been
Anybody quite like them.

TO BE SOMEWHERE ELSE

I want to go
To the beach
I want to feel
The sun on my skin
And the sand
Between my toes
And the waves
Washing up my leg
I want to feel
The breeze by the sea
I want to feel care free
Careless, even
Sometimes
I couldn't care less
For all the things around me
All the things that hold me
All the things I'm committed to
Freedom
Is much more priceless
And a beautiful idea
I wish I was there
Instead of here
I wish the grind
Wasn't necessary

I wish I didn't have to
Spend time around people
Who wouldn't look twice at me
In the street
Who wouldn't even
Pour water on me
If I was on fire
It's not a great way
To spend your time
In confined spaces
Around people
Who tolerate you
Rather than celebrate you
People who gossip in corners
Unaware
That they were gossiped about too
Every time they leave the room
And laughed at
I laugh at that
It's funny to me
Anywhere, but here
Somewhere
Is where I'd rather be
I long to feel
The sun on my skin again
Walking along the beach

Without a care
To be here or there
And what a tragedy
To be where you are
Longing
To be somewhere else
What a tragedy
For peace of mind
What a tragedy for self
But nevertheless
It's something to hope for
Something to set sights on
Inside the mind
Something to motivate
Something to set designs upon
A place far away from here
A place there
Somewhere
In blue water
Under the sun.

TRAVEL PLANS

I think what I'd like to do
Is plan
For a couple of years
And save up
For my next big trip
I'm not sure where yet
But I know
The main things I need to do
Is save the money
And give it a couple of years
To do that
And meanwhile
Plan where I want to go
And then book it
Or the other way around
I don't know where yet
But that's what I want to do
I think I want to go somewhere
For perhaps a month
Maybe six weeks
And just explore
Travel to maybe a few places
In that time
I think that's the way I want to do it

Not just a two week holiday there
A week holiday here
I want to do it a bit differently
And I'm going to be reaching
That milestone age as well
So some kind of way
Of marking that milestone
Some way of celebrating it
I think that's what I want to do
I just don't know where yet
But I'm thinking about it
And what places
I might want to go to
Within that time
One big travel trip
A month
To six weeks
And just go
And be gone
And explore
And see some places
That I haven't seen before
Experience some things
That I haven't experienced
Add on some excursions to it as well
Go and do some of those

Do some off the beaten track stuff as well
That's what I would like to do in my head
That's what I've been thinking about
For like a year or so now
I think that's really what I want to do
Something very different.

WHAT WE HAD

You'll miss me
So bad
And it won't be about sex
It'll be beyond that
You'll miss my eyes
That you believe
Have said more
Than I actually did
Your hands
Will miss
Holding my hands
It will be every touch
Your lips
Will miss mine
That sense of
Belonging to someone
You'll miss
All the happy times with me
You're not happy now
And won't be
Until you hear my heart
So many things
Can happen in a week
You'll miss me

To listen to you
You'll miss my voice
And my words
That became your friend
A year before you met me
You didn't need to see me
Or talk to me
That seemed
To keep you happy
You won't be happy
And at peace
Not speaking to me
Not hearing me speak to you
Not knowing
What's inside me
Knowing
I have no shortage of words
Now you wait
And learn patience
You who were always in a rush
You will wait to hear
You will write
Though you said
You won't
You will call again
To hear from me

You'll want to do it
You'll want to apologise
For all the messages
And for all the mess
That you created
Saying
There's no bad intentions
That you're not a bad human
And that your actions
Were purely caused
Out of the fear
Of losing
What we had.

WHY WOMEN CHEAT

Why does a woman cheat
That's a damned good question
I have cheated, she said
And have been cheated on
She believes there's
Many different reasons
Why a woman cheats
One million reasons maybe
Once when she was drunk
At a Christmas party
She had a quickie
He was handsome
Paid her the right compliments
And she was horny
The following day
She almost forgot all about it
And there lays the cover up, she said
As the partner
You will never find out
Because everything
Is back to normal the following day
Also, she said
When the relationship
Has become a routine

No intimacy
Physically
Emotionally
Having a wondering eye
A woman
Can become attracted
To another man
And start an affair
But doesn't want to leave the partner
Because she maybe
Hopes for better days
Financial security
And truly loves her partner
Here again lays the cover up
I have been those women, she said
Admittedly
I believe that as human beings
A part you
Is controlled by your instincts
And due to narcissistic tendencies
I can cheat if I want
And deny it from now
Until judgement day
In general, she said
Women are exceptionally good at lying
I am admitting to that.

WOMEN OF CONSEQUENCE

I want to say
That I really do appreciate
A woman
Who is in her faith
She has belief in God
Having been with women
Who have no belief in God
Having gone through that
I really appreciate
When there is a woman
Who without any doubt
Sees it the other way
She does think
There are consequences
To her actions
And that God is watching.

YEARNING FOR YOU

I woke up longing
The night wrapped around me
It's your body that I need
Your skin, your breath, your heat
I wish you were here now
Beneath me, and needy
Your warm soft thighs wide open
Your bright eyes drowsy with want
I'd kiss you so intensely, but slowly
Everywhere, like God made you to be
Until you arch towards me
Wanting me more and more
Needing me deep inside you
And I wouldn't stop going
Until you were trembling for sure
With your hips rising with desire
To meet my every stroke
Until you're grasping, and gasping
Saying my name like you own me
Or as if proclaiming that you're mine
As our bodies tighten and we climax
And we finally come undone
And we lay there truly satisfied
Falling asleep 'til we meet the sun.

THE AUTHOR

Phoenix James is an award winning Writer, Poet, Author and Spoken Word Recording Artist. He began performing his poetic words live on stages across the UK in 1998. His debut spoken word poetry album, The A.R.T.I.S.T, was released in 2000. His first limited edition printed collection of poetry, To Whom It May Concern, was published in 2003. He has toured and performed his poetry internationally since 2004. He has appeared in films, on television and radio shows, and collaborated with other artists, singer-songwriters, actors, musicians, filmmakers and producers. In 2013, he wrote, directed and produced the feature length mock documentary film, Love Freely but Pay for Sex. Phoenix James is the author of several poetry collections and has recorded and released several spoken word poetry albums including Phenzwaan Now & Forever, A Patchwork Remedy for A Broken Melody, FREE, Haven for the Tormented, With All That Said, Light Beams from the Void, and over sixty spoken word poetry singles. All are available online now and streaming everywhere worldwide.

If you enjoyed reading this book, please leave a review or comment online. The author reads every review and they help new readers discover and experience his work.

PHOENIX JAMES

Photo by Phoenix James

Phoenix James lives in London, England.

Connect with Phoenix James online via his
social media platforms and let others know that
you've been fortunate to discover this book.
To contact or learn more about Phoenix James
and his creative journey or to receive updates
via his Newsletter Mailing List, visit his official
website at www.PhoenixJamesOfficial.com

CHECK OUT THE AUTHOR'S OTHER
BOOK TITLES ALSO AVAILABLE
IN PAPERBACK & EBOOK

PHOENIX JAMES
POETRY & SPOKEN WORD
COLLECTIONS:

LOVE, SEX, ROMANCE & OTHER BAD THINGS

ROUTE TO DESTRUCTION

DELIRIUM OF THE WISE

DON'T LET THE DAFFODILS FOOL YOU

CALL ME WHEN YOU'RE FREE

FAR FROM THE OUTSIDE

THE ONES WE DIDN'T KILL

LESSONS FROM EVERYWHERE

ANOTHER ONE FOR BURNING

A LONG BRIGHT COLD DARK SUMMER

SHAME POINT ZERO

THE SANDBAG THEORY

SOFT, SEXY & WET

BELOW BASE LEVEL

TO CATCH A PASSING UFO

DISCOVER THESE AND MUCH MORE AT
PHOENIXJAMESOFFICIAL.COM

Phoenix James Official

www.ingramcontent.com/pod-product-compliance
Lightning Source LLC
Chambersburg PA
CBHW021237090426
42740CB00006B/580

*9 7 8 1 0 6 8 5 3 8 3 1 5 *